21 Days

Catherine Lima

BookLeaf Publishing

Presentation by *BookLeaf Publishing*

Web: www.bookleafpub.com

E-mail: info@bookleafpub.com

ISBN: 9789357442527

First edition 2023

To you. Yes, you.

ACKNOWLEDGEMENT

I have a collection of poems in different journals that I have kept since I was 21 years old. I have loved writing since even before I knew how to spell my own name. I remember, right before going into kindergarten, just grabbing a pen and scribbling circles thinking that I was writing.

I never thought I'd see the day when I finally got the opportunity to have my poems published. I am very thankful to BookLeaf Publishing, for allowing me to fulfill this dream of mine.

I am also thankful for my family, who has kept me grounded throughout all these years and for supporting me. It has been a very long and weary journey, but it doesn't end here. This is my first step at becoming the poet I've always wanted to be.

Lastly, I am thankful for anyone who decided to take a peak inside and I hope that my words have some type of impact.

Hazy

It all seems kind of hazy -
almost like a dream.
At times I feel I'm crazy -
what could this all mean?

The Calling

It is in this seat in which you call to me.
I sit and stare out into space.
I feel you next to me.

Time moves on, yet I am here and
Think about the time I've lost.

The leaves fall down with the breeze, and
Time stands still.

The sun shines down, but
Gloomy entities within my mind -
they bring me down beside.

The storm, it booms inside my skull.
Raindrops fall into my eyes.
For me to understand this pain - I don't think I
ever will.

Oh, how hard it is to live without a friendly
voice to hear,
without a chest to hold my fragile heart, it aches.
For it to feel, again -
for it to feel once more.
For it to heal, again -
for it to heal once more.

Thankfully Pleased

Today, the weather is a gloom.
The sun peaks through the clouds.
The birds all sing the song of waking up to life.

This day is born for me.
I am at ease.
I am at peace.

I can see clearly who I will come to be.
I am thankful.
I am pleased

The Loud Silence

My mind - it swirls
with thoughts from yesterday.
Helplessly - I feel
as if I have no choice.

My thoughts are as loud as silence.
A pin drops to the ground, and
briefly they come to a halt.

In motion - they continue.
Hastily - they travel.

Puffing out smoke, and chugging away.
Stopped in their tracks now.

My thoughts are at crossroads -
which path will I take?

BOOM!

My thoughts are as loud as silence.

Me Too

Sucked inside your mind -
you are hiding from the

Truth be told - it hurts, but
it shall set you free from

You - the only enemy inside
your mind - it grows

With pain from deep within
your heart - it aches

To love once more - it hurts
your eyes, I know

This pain - it is all too
familiar to me, too.

Me, too.

Past/Present

I'm not as young as I used to be,
but I still feel the same.

Maybe someday I'll get used to this,
before I go insane.

Tired of Today

I am tired of today,
I wish for it to end.

To start again tomorrow,
seems much too far away.

I am tired of today.
I wish to wilt away.

To end it all right now,
is much too complicated.

I want to run away, and
fall to death's sweet grace.

…but I won't.

I can't.

I am just tired of today.

I wish to sleep, but
I keep on waking up.

Drowning

I am an anchor,
sinking deeper and deeper.

Who can bring me to the surface?
Not I. No.

I need help.
Who is there?
I call out.
No one cares.

It's hard to breathe.
I am drowning.
My vision blurs,
through liquid form.

I can't move.
I'm stuck.
I've drowned.
I'm gone.

My World

I feel most at ease
when I am at home.
I block the world around me, and
enter in my own.

I step foot into a dimension
that no one else can see.
As I may have mentioned
this is when I'm at ease.

My mind goes blank.
There is a stare.
I forget.
What despair.

Self Reflection

I don't know who you are, and
you don't know who I am.

Maybe someday we'll cross paths.

I see the world not as myself, but
I don't know who she is.

She's afraid.
She's shy.
She's quiet.
She's delicate.
She's young.
She's….me?

A broken child with tears and fears.

I hold her tightly in my heart, and
I miss her so.

She was brave.
She was active.
She was sharp.
She was strong.
She was a child.
She was…me.

I see the world not as it is, but
it’s dark and cold.

I am tired and
I wish to sleep.

I am awake and
I am alive, but
I am not fine.

Catch Up

I hope that I get life
before it gets to me.
For it will be the
death of me.

I feel as if I'm drifting
out into the sea.
I have no destination
or sense of direction.

I am on an odyssey, and
the captain of my own ship.
I don't have a crew, but
the sun and the moon.

I can't help but wonder –
How would my life seem?
Had I not forgotten
who I was born to be.

Daydream

Puffy eyes,
And sunset skies.

The clouds above
Fill me with love.

All around
The leaves will fall.

Raindrops kiss
The floor with bliss.

Take my hand
And leave this land.

Maybe one day
Peace will exist.

Thirteen

Unlucky number thirteen
how this number follows me.
It calls to me through
the whispers in the wind.

Lucky number thirteen
how this number welcomes me.
It leads me right into
the wonders of the world.

Clear

There is a breeze, and
the sun shines bright.
The air is fresh, and
I take a breath.

I breathe in, and
it feels great.
I breathe out,
without a doubt.

My mind-
It clears.

Keeping Up

This lingering sadness
is a wandering presence.

Keeping a straight face, and
keeping up with the pace.

I Look through the window, and
there's a crack in the view.

Keeping myself sane, and
keeping up with a plane.

A Day like Today

A day like today
is like no other.

The sun shines bright
above the sky.

The air is crisp
with a hint of last night's soul.

A day like today
is like no other.

It brings us hope
that there will be another.

The air is as sweet as the breath of life
that I received from my mother.

Alone, Again

So here I sit alone, again
year after year.

But at least I indulge in
all of life’s different flavors.

With a sip and a breath
and a taste and a touch.

At least I am alive.

Ode to the Earth

The weather changes
as do I.
It's hot one day, and
cold the next.

How blind we are
to make a change.
How sad it is that
we kill ourselves.

My head – it hurts
from tears produced.
My mind – soon shuts
with apathy.

It's hard to see
through the smoggy air.
It's hard to breathe in
the toxic fumes.

The Earth – it grows
through the broken cracks.
I hope one day
the Earth will rise.

Stuck

There is a bright, lit path before me.
Still, I choose the path behind me.
I dream of fears and disappointment.
I wake to feelings of resentment.

I follow my heart as best as I can
though, I still end up breaking it.
What is this pain I feel inside?
Will it ever go away?

A broken vase can be restored, but
still the cracks are fresh.
Still the sound it made is there
floating 'round the air.

Silently - I listen to the whispers of
your voice inside of me.
Carefully, I choose the words
I wish to speak to you.

Wandering

My mind wanders into
depths unseen by me.

Carefully, I watch as
thoughts turn into plays.

I try to find my way, but
I keep running into yesterday.

I keep on wandering,
wondering where I went wrong.

Life

I am moving forward, but
something brings me back.

The trust I have in you.
The trust you have in me.

That's what keeps me going.

Sometimes it gets scary.
Sometimes I stay still.

How can I move forward,
when my feet are stuck?

As I roam along this earth, and
follow the path set for me.
As I find my voice, now
I can understand what it means to live.

www.ingramcontent.com/pod-product-compliance
Lightning Source LLC
Chambersburg PA
CBHW051716130826
49812CB00034B/1216
* 9 7 8 9 3 5 7 4 4 2 5 2 7 *